GW00402060

Todd
and Learning

by

Ken Adams

EGMONT WORLD LIMITED

"The National Society for the Prevention of Cruelty to Children (NSPCC) has a vision – a society where all children are loved, valued and able to fulfil their potential. The NSPCC is pleased to work with Egmont World Limited on the development of this series of child care guides. We believe that they will help parents and carers better understand children's and babies' needs.'

Jim Harding, Chief Executive, NSPCC.

Designer: Dave Murray
Illustrator: John Haslam
Editor: Stephanie Sloan
Cover design: Craig Cameron
Front cover photograph supplied
by Telegraph Colour LIbrary

Copyright © 2000 Egmont World Limited. All rights reserved.
Published in Great Britain in 2000 by Egmont World Limited,
a division of Egmont Holding Limited,
Deanway Technology Centre, Wilmslow Road, Handforth,
Cheshire, SK9 3FB. Printed in Italy
ISBN 0 7498 4776 X
A catalogue record for this book is available
from the British Library.

Toddler talk and learning

by Ken Adams

Contents

Introduction

This book is for parents and other adults who have the care of toddlers. We use the word "toddler" to refer to young children who have started to walk and are able to say a few real words. For the purposes of this book a toddler is a child between the ages of 14 months to 4 years old. Toddlers have a need to *know* about their world, to be creative, to talk about how and why, to be read to, to sing songs, dance and act out stories. A parent who has concern for a child's needs will want to know how to satisfy them, by providing practical experiences, by reading rhymes, riddles, songs and stories, and by visiting places of interest. There will be choices of toys and books to make, and knowledge of what objects around the house can further a toddler's understanding and development.

Note:
The activities mentioned in this book should always be supervised by the parent or carer. If you know that your child has special needs you may need to adapt the activities accordingly.

The parent-child interactions quoted in this book are taken from the author's own experiences, both as a parent of four children and as a teacher.

When referring to the child, we have alternated the use of he and she throughout the book.

CHAPTER 1

Toddler talking activities

Your toddler is learning to talk and communicate with you when she begins to repeat and make up sounds.

Talking for toddlers can be helped by:

- mouthing and saying words directly to a small child;
- talking in a simplistic way about objects, everyday happenings or events;
- reading a picture book to her, or reciting nursery rhymes;
- giving clear instructions;
- answering the many questions that an older toddler often asks;
- using a wide variety of play activities as detailed in this book.

First words

Babies and toddlers first learn to speak by copying the sounds and words that their parents say, particularly if they are repeated over and over again.

Tiffany's auntie tried this with her, when she was a very young baby indeed. You could see Tiffany staring intently at her auntie, at the actions of mouth and tongue, making an effort to copy the inflexions and sounds that were being made in saying "hello". This suggests that a baby or toddler learns quickest from studying the *way* you say words, as well as the sounds you make. So, when talking to a baby or toddler, it will help if you face her and speak the words clearly, so that she can see *how* you form the words and make the sounds.

Concrete words

These are simple nouns.

They are the easiest words for a child to grasp, because they refer to real-life objects. Start with simple concrete words – cup, plate, potty, mouth, hair, nose – pointing to the object as the word is said. How often a word needs to be repeated in a period is best guided by a baby's or toddler's interest.

When a word or words are repeated, a parent can be guided by what daily activity baby is taking part in. At dinner-time, a parent can say "spoon", "dish" or "cup"; when getting dressed it might be "shoe" or "socks". There need be no formal attempt to teach or emphasise such words. Talking to a toddler is a part of everyday life.

Gaining attention

A good way to direct attention to what you say is,

for example, to hold up the object near to your face, when you say "jumper" at dressing-time, so that your child can see the way you speak and form the word. This is even easier at mealtimes, because a parent often sits near to a toddler while she eats, and can point out objects. This should not be overdone, though, because concentrating on eating is far more important than making word sounds.

Baby talk

Speaking to a baby or toddler in made-up half- or part- words can be surprisingly useful in the early stages of talking. Since a toddler learns by copying mouth and tongue formations, and the sounds that accompany them, even "cootchie-coo", "boo-boo" and other endearments are very useful.

Such made-up words are a useful preliminary to actual word-making, as long as Mum or Dad can break the habit from time to time and say real words. In general, made-up words are used in fun, and the enjoyment transmits from parent to child, making a toddler relaxed and happy to take part in such "games".

Instructions

As soon as possible, it is wise to speak useful words, including instructions such as "eat", "drink", "come here" and "sit down". Single words, accompanied by actions to emphasise the point, can be replaced by two or three words, sometimes even from the beginning. Instruction words are extremely important, and a parent needs to inform of danger apart from continually saying "no!" or "don't!" For example, a parent might say "hot!" or "burn!" with accompanying actions and facial expressions, when a toddler tries to drink or touch a hot mug or teacup.

This sort of instruction led to Mark toddling round the room repeating to himself, over and over, "oooo, hot!" and "oooo, burn!" At least he got the message!

Speaking in sentences

Toddlers quickly progress to speaking short sentences, often grammatically incorrect, like "want drink", "give me" and "me dolly". This is a natural transition phase, and a parent needs to continue talking in his or her own clearly expressed sentences. As time passes, a toddler picks up the core words in the sentences that you speak. Speaking to him or her as naturally as you would to an older child also encourages a toddler in talking.

Other incentives to talking

There are other ways to encourage talking. You can talk about something interesting that has happened, something he or she has seen on TV, or in a book. As a toddler, John knew what a bridge was, and had an idea about "gold". So, when he saw a picture of the Golden Gate Bridge in San Francisco, his eyes opened wide: "Is it really gold?" he asked.

At a certain point in time, some toddlers with very enquiring minds do not need to be encouraged to talk. They ask questions continually, and about everything. In spite of a barrage of such questions, it is important that you try to answer most of what is asked, otherwise she can become frustrated, even making up her own answers. It is important, of course, to generate interest. Stories and nursery rhymes have a magic all their own, and toddlers very often respond fervently, particularly if you act out a story, or sing a rhyme. Chris, in particular, is fascinated by the "acting out" of the giant in a fairy story, or the singing of "round and round the garden". They are a source of endless fun and deep enjoyment.

Taking your child to the supermarket, the seaside, or a zoo, reading books, reading to her, saying nursery rhymes, giving instructions – all give her vital encouragement to talk.

Slow to talk

A child may not say words immediately, but there is no cause for alarm. Many slow-to-start talkers often pick up quickly, catch up with other children, and even excel academically later in life.

However, if you, as a parent, are concerned, then see your health visitor, family GP, or contact one of the relevant agencies mentioned at the end of this book.

CHAPTER 2

Learning through investigative play

A playful approach to learning is important because it will stimulate interest and aid concentration. Play is a toddler's way of learning about the world, so allow her to take the lead and respect her need to assert her independence.

Investigative play includes:

• water play (floating, sinking);
• sand play (space);
• the air about us (blowing, sucking);
• in the garden;
• mechanical things (wind up toys, pedal cars);
• weighing and balancing;
• using the senses;
• fruit and vegetables.

Water play

Jackie plays at the sink every day. She puts on a little plastic apron and, with a sink full of tepid water, plays with plastic toys, plastic cups and spoons in the water.

For a toddler, the attractions of water are many. It can be splashed. It can be poured from one plastic cup to another. Some objects sink, others float. The games are endless, and the very fundamental ideas of science gained from such play are invaluable.

There is also similar 'play' in the bath, and here there are bubbles to investigate as well. Different-sized plastic cups are important for bath or sink play, because he can then find out about filling a big cup from a smaller one. There are many words to learn, and for you to talk about together: water, float, sink, fill, big, small, bigger, smaller, wet, dry.

Sand play

A large cat-litter tray filled with sand incorporates similar play to water play, without the tendency a toddler has to develop everything into a splashing

and displacement exercise. Sand can be used to fill different-sized plastic cups. When it is wet, it can be used for modelling (although this particular activity is better done on a separate wooden board).

Both sand and water play teach important concepts such as floating and sinking, capacity, that water can change shape, without putting an abstract label to these ideas.

The air about us

Very important ideas in science come from early play with straws and balloons, and by talking about moving air, such as wind.

For a young toddler, play with balloons and bubbles gives the idea that air can possess some force. You can blow up a couple of balloons for your toddler to play with, or blow bubbles for him to chase.

Blowing through a straw shows that air can have force, and can fan the face or move hair, just like wind. Bubbles and balloons float to a certain extent, and do not fall like toys dropped from the hand.

These are things to talk about, but not to labour over. The practical activities that a toddler tries at this age are simply laying down experience upon which later abstract thinking is based, and can be investigated at a much older age.

In the garden

You will probably not have to introduce your toddler to investigating things in the garden. Many a toddler has wandered into the house, clutching an earthworm or a ladybird, enquiring:

"Look, what this?"

After spelling out the dangers of bees and wasps, and of eating leaves and berries from bushes, there are many things to collect and talk about in the garden:

- stones of various shapes and sizes;
- small insects;
- daisies, fallen leaves.

Try to make your garden a safe place to play, e.g. by covering any ponds, or trimming back low branches from trees. After a toddler has looked at things in the garden, it becomes more interesting for him to be shown pictures from books on insects, flowers and trees. This becomes a very important topic for discussion, with an older toddler in particular.

Mechanical things

Science investigations at school will benefit from your toddler having first explored harmless mechanical objects, such as old watches and clocks, toy cars, etc.

Toy cars, in particular, can be used in all kinds of play activities. Allowing metal cars to run down a slope, and seeing how far they run, is actually looking at the effects of gravity and friction, without spelling out such complexities. The winding up of an old watch or clock, with the back removed, shows how cogs interact and a spring tightens. The language of communication of such things does not need to be more than very simplistic, because it is the practical experience of observation which is important.

Weighing things

A toy balance, of the see-saw variety, can illustrate simple concepts like 'heavy', 'light' and 'same'.

For a young toddler, it is best to show how to put small toys, such as marbles, on to the weighing pans, and then leave him to experiment. An older toddler might like more parental input, with you showing and explaining. For example, through using marbles to weigh his toys, a toddler will find it surprising that some small metal toys are heavier than larger teddy bears!

Using the senses

Play activities in this area include:

• sight;   • hearing;   • touch;   • taste;   • smell.

Sight play involves games for an older toddler such as "I spy with my little eye", which can be applied to things like colour: "I spy with my little eye, a colour beginning with y", yellow being the colour of some object in the room. Obviously, he must know some colours before this can be attempted. Another game is to place two or three toys on the table, ask the toddler to take note of them, then cover with a cloth to see if he remembers them. This game improves memory, and leads a toddler to greater confidence in himself, as long as only a small number of objects at a time are hidden.

Hearing

Try asking your toddler to close his eyes, then ring a bell or clap your hands, or play on a toy xylophone, asking him to name the object. This is an activity for a slightly older toddler. If you want to try this with a younger child, choose only those sounds that he is very familiar with.

Touch

You can play similar games by asking your child to close his eyes and try to identify objects by touch, e.g. certain toys, dolls, teddies, a cup, spoon, plate.

Taste and smell

This needs to involve objects that a toddler can *easily* recognise by taste and smell, while he closes his eyes, e.g. an apple, an orange (taste and smell), Mum's perfume (smell).

Fruits and vegetables

Look at a variety of different fruits and vegetables, e.g. apples, pears, tomatoes, bananas, grapes, carrots, potatoes, cabbages, together. Cut them open to show the seeds and, for an older toddler, talk about where they are grown. You could grow cress seeds on a saucer of damp cotton wool.

Toys to help investigations

- Child's balance scales;
- Play clocks.

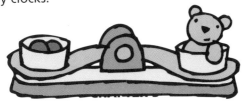

CHAPTER 3

Learning through imaginative play

The value of imaginative and role play should not be underestimated. In such play, a toddler is acting out what she sees in real life, trying and testing the limits of what is possible, without harm coming to her. She is also learning to express inner feelings and to satisfy her creative drive.

Learning through imaginative play involves:

- listening to songs and rhymes, and banging or clapping in time to music;
- learning to sing simple rhymes and songs from parents, tapes, TV, CD-ROMS;
- using saucepans and other utensils as musical instruments;
- dressing up and acting out rhymes, fairy stories and nursery songs;
- dancing to music of all types – children's songs, pop music, Disney songs, classical music;
- using dolls and teddy bears in role play;
- real-life and imaginative play, using a variety of toys including postman, nurse, doctor outfits and garage, airport, zoo, farm toys.

Nursery rhymes and songs

Nursery rhymes and songs can lead to very adventurous imaginative play by toddlers. They can sing along with Mum or Dad, copy their actions, and dance to recordings on tape. Reading nursery rhymes and fairy stories leads to play with dolls, and dressing up to act out the story.

Hannah dresses up as fairy-tale characters. She has been read stories at bedtime for a year now, and she loves to talk about the pictures and sing along with the rhymes. In her play she lines up her dolls and teddy bears, and takes them through her favourite story of the moment. One week the biggest teddy is the giant, and a doll is Jack. For an older toddler (three years old), she is very inventive. She speaks for them both in words she

has heard over and over again at bedtime readings. On another day, she favours Billy Goats Gruff, and builds her play around that story. She loves dressing up and becoming a character in a story, particularly if she is with other toddlers, who she organises with ruthless efficiency!

More music

Young toddlers will listen to tapes, watch stories enacted on TV, or on CD-ROM. They will move in time to music, or get up and dance. At two years old, John stands on the sofa and dances to music. Zanub stands on the spot clicking her tongue in time to the music, jigging up and down. Others prefer to make their own music, using wooden spoons, saucepans and saucepan lids to create sounds. If your toddler enjoys music, a toy xylophone or trumpet would be a good buy.

Dressing up

A large box full of old clothes can be very useful. An older toddler will use hats, shoes, jumpers, shirts and dresses in role play, to play Mummy or Daddy, or some part in a story that has been read to him or her. This is often an important part of a fun and active child's play.

Anne was always dressing up, and in later student life found a place at a top London drama school. The old clothes for her box came from adult and child cast-offs, from jumble sales and village fêtes. Anne used them for many years, from being a toddler to a six- or seven-year-old.

Music and dancing

Movement to all types of music is very much a toddler delight. Whether you provide pop, classical, children's songs or a song from Disney's *The Lion King*, your toddler will gain greatly from dancing, especially if Mum, Dad, or brothers and sisters join in.

Real-life and imaginary play with toys

Real-life play easily merges into imaginary play when a toddler plays with dolls, uses a playmat to run cars over pretend roads, or dresses up as a policeman or nurse.

An older toddler may be happy to play on her own, copying what she knows about in real-life and embellishing it with imaginary behaviour. She will play with a garage and experiment with language: "Brrm. Fill up. Brrm."

The toddler nurse will treat the teddy patient, copying what she sees on TV, or has seen at the clinic. The tone is clearly borrowed from what she has heard: "Lie still, naughty, naughty, behave. Go sleep," says Jenny.

Talking from imaginative play

This comes from role play, copying the language and behaviour of adults, extended with the toddler's own additions. She listens to the words of rhymes, and sings and repeats them:

> Humpty Dumpty sat on a wall,
> Humpty Dumpty had a great fall ...

A toddler learns word meanings through play. For example, opposites can be learned from the actions you use to demonstrate what happens when Humpty Dumpty *falls* down (your hand movements showing direction).

Another example is:

> Incy Wincy Spider, climbing *up* the spout
> *Down* came the rain and washed the spider out.

When the toddler repeats the rhyme, she often repeats the actions as well as the words.

Musical games

Stop-start

Apart from toy xylophones, mouth organs, drums and assorted instruments that can be bought, the kitchen will yield saucepans to bang, sieves to run wooden spoons across, and plastic bottles to half-fill with water and blow across the top of. Tell your child that you want her to play until you bang a ruler loudly on the table. At first you may have to accompany this signal with "stop now".

Musical statues

A variation is to play music and tell your child to dance, and when the music stops, to stop and stand still – like a statue. This game is best played in a group.

Loud and quiet

Ask your child to play loudly and quietly when you say.

Lower and higher

Ask her to copy you singing a nursery rhyme. Then tell her to copy as you sing higher, then lower.

CHAPTER 4

Learning through creative play

Creative play for toddlers of all ages involves different types of drawing, colouring and craft work:

- using thick crayons to draw lines, and to colour-in spaces and shapes;
- finger painting and, later, using a thick brush to paint meaningful pictures;
- using Plasticine and similar materials for very basic modelling;
- sticking coloured shapes on to large sheets of paper;
- potato-printing and using other shapes to make creative designs on paper;
- building using wooden or plastic bricks, or interlocking bricks;
- using coloured chalks on blackboards.

Crayoning

This is a very useful way to begin. Small fingers cope best with thick crayons, so use these at first, and show your toddler how to draw coloured lines on a sheet of white paper. Then show him how to produce different colours with different coloured crayons. Essentially, this should be a very free activity. Don't be surprised at the number of large sheets of paper that a toddler can get through!

As your toddler becomes more competent at using a crayon, you can show him how to draw wiggly lines, curves and circles. Later still, he can try to draw a cross, and use thinner crayons. Older toddlers might prefer to use pencil crayons, although this is a more advanced skill. You need to move along as your toddler becomes more naturally proficient. Colouring-in defined spaces usually needs the skills of an older small child. When he is able to do this, colouring can be a very satisfying activity indeed.

Different types of painting
It is best to use water-based, washable paint. Young toddlers find it difficult to handle a paintbrush. Paint seems to get itself in the hair

and all over the face as much as on the paper! Finger painting is an easier option. He simply dips his fingers in the paint, and makes coloured patterns on the paper. Alternatively, you can use potato halves, sponges, wooden animal shapes, even toy cars, dipped into paint and used to print coloured shapes on paper.

Later, your toddler will take to using a paintbrush, which needs to be short-handled and thick, initially. Later, different types of brush can be experimented with.

Clearly, painting can be a messy business, and it is wise to spread newspaper over the floor, table and chair to catch dripping paint. The would-be Monet should be dressed in old clothes, or wear an apron.

Anne looked forward to this part of the day. "Want paint!" she demanded, at the beginning of every morning.

Something that makes a toddler feel very proud is to stick his works of art on the bedroom or kitchen wall. "These are your *best* paintings," I said to John. He snuggled down in the bedclothes, a little smile on his face, and lay there staring lovingly at what he had produced.

Plasticine and modelling

First attempts at modelling are often with Plasticine and Play-doh. This may involve simply breaking off bits of one colour and sticking them on to another colour until the Plasticine is one multicoloured ball.

Two years later the same toddler will be more discriminating, trying to make little men or animals with green legs and red bodies. At that point your input is to show your toddler how to roll out and shape the modelling materials in different ways.

Sticking coloured shapes

This activity can be highly creative. Sadia sits and carefully considers exactly where each shape will be placed on the paper, relative to all the others. She is expressing and developing her toddler design sense. A lot of mental effort and thinking goes into what she does, and to her the

creation of coloured stars on a white background is very important.

Coloured chalks

These can be messy, but have the advantage that they can be used both on paper and on a blackboard surface. A toddler can work at the table or stand at the blackboard. Be ready to help a young toddler, and work with him on chalk play. An older toddler is best left to experiment, after a short explanation from you.

Creative craft toys

For this age group, building with bricks is highly engrossing. There are various types of brick that a toddler can play with, for example ordinary play bricks (preferably wooden), and various types of interlocking bricks, which need to be pushed together. There are also light, over-sized plastic bricks which are useful for building "walls" and "houses".

Creative toys for toddlers

It really is worth investing in these toys for your toddler:

• wooden bricks;
• boxes of play shapes;
• oversized plastic 3-D shapes;
• plasticine and play-doh.

CHAPTER 5

Early maths activities

For a toddler these include:

- counting (small numbers of objects) such as buttons or marbles;
- using an abacus, towers of bricks, trains of bricks;
- recognising numbers (on houses, buses);
- copying a circle, drawing a cross (older toddler);
- sorting – spoons from forks, cups and saucers, socks into piles (for colours and patterns), building brick shapes;
- simple jigsaws – 5 pieces (for some toddlers).

Counting

Counting real-life objects is one of the most natural learning activities for toddlers. When you take your toddler for a walk along the road, to the supermarket, on a bus or train trip, or in the car, there are many things to see and count. There are houses, cars, bicycles, men, women, tins, packets of cereal, loaves of bread. Sitting in the supermarket trolley, James had to stop and count every few minutes: "One, two, three … one, two, three … one, two, three …".

Toddlers learn to count lower numbers of objects first – one, two, three – then up to five, and on to ten. In general, they learn naturally and easily, and with great enjoyment. There is no need for you to hurry the learning of spoken numbers, or to rush on to bigger numbers. A good abacus is an invaluable aid, or your toddler can practise counting with buttons.

Recognising written numbers

Anne asks about written numbers continually: "What house that?" "Nineteen," says Mum. "What number that?" Mum tells her, "Seventy-nine." Anne is interested in the numbers (and letters) she sees along the road and in shops, but she will not learn much about associating shape with certain numbers. She recognises, for example, the shape of the numerals 2 and 8, but nothing else. The need to *know* is very strong indeed.

Copying with a crayon

Thick crayons are a must for toddlers, used on a large sheet of white or light-coloured paper. A toddler can often draw straight or curved lines, sometimes a circle. Crosses are harder for them, as are square shapes.

You can draw lines, circles, rectangles and crosses on the sheet, then allow your child to experiment using a variety of thick, coloured crayons. Expertise increases with age, even without practice.

Sorting

This is another practical activity that can stimulate a toddler's intellect in an enjoyable way. The sorting of coloured objects is particularly useful. Children's play bricks can be sorted into groups of two or three colours, for example, red, blue and yellow bricks. Bricks can also be sorted for shape as well as colour, and for size.

Spoons and forks put into a pile will entertain a toddler for some time, as she sorts and separates them into two piles. You will need to demonstrate this. Some toddlers seem more interested in building patterns around themselves, or making sounds by banging spoons together, than in sorting them into groups. This is important for the child, so a parent needs to bow to her desire to experiment. Trying to direct your child in a particular direction will lead to frustration.

Matching

This is a slightly more difficult activity for a toddler: laying the table, matching knife with fork, and cup with saucer. Matching socks from an assorted pile demands good recognition of patterns *and* colours. However, matching practice is well within the capability of an older toddler, who can find it very enjoyable indeed. Anne is often found sitting in the middle of the living room, sorting out socks or clothes into two or three piles. "Daddy's socks … Mummy's socks … Baby's socks …" and so on.

Jigsaws

Older toddlers achieve some success with four- or five-piece jigsaws, but find larger numbers of pieces difficult and frustrating to do. When she is old enough, jigsaw puzzles help to improve shape recognition and manual dexterity. Like all these practical or play activities, though, your child needs to enjoy them in a relaxed way, seeking to satisfy natural curiosity, and to learn through enjoyment.

Talking in maths activities

Any practical or play activity that a parent introduces to a child lends itself to communication and, inevitably, communication by the spoken word:

Mum:　"Look at this. Try this," or "Look, I'm putting the bricks one on top of the other. One ... two ... three," and "You do it!"

Toddler: "Me do it," and "one ... two ..." then "brick " and "jicksaw", "socks ... lellow."

At first, as this book illustrates, every activity is a talking activity.

CHAPTER 6
Reading to your child

There are many books that can be used to introduce the joys of reading to a toddler. These include:

- board books and bath books;
- finger rhymes;
- nursery rhymes;
- nursery and children's songs;
- simply told fairy stories;
- CD-ROMS, videos, TV stories;
- picture books;
- highly pictorial information books.

Toddlers enjoy several elements when being read to. They include:

- rhythm and rhyme;
- acting out characters in a story;
- pictures to talk about.

Board and bath books
These have pictures and, usually, a word or two, or even no words at all. Essentially, they are for you to look at and talk about with your toddler. They introduce books, and interesting things in books.

They are also fairly indestructible, like many plastic toys.

Hannah carried her board book of farmyard animals everywhere with her, and that meant *everywhere*, in the bathroom, the garden, the supermarket, and walking around the zoo. It was her favourite "toy".

When introducing a young toddler to books it is very important that first books are an enjoyable "toy". It is a time when Mum or Dad pays attention to their child, talks about the pictures in the book, acts out part of a story, or even makes the noise of the farmyard animal shown on the page.

Bedtime, in particular, is "read-a-story-time," and "talk about the pictures in my book time," or even finger-rhyme time. However, many finger rhymes fit in better with daytime activities, because they often involve tickling, which rather stirs a toddler to activity rather than settling him or her down to sleep.

Finger Rhymes

These are very simple rhyming songs, often started in babyhood, but continued for a toddler, if only for the fact that older pre-school children enjoy them so much. They include "This little piggy went to market", "Round and round the garden"

and "This little finger, this little toe". They are not necessarily 'talk-about' rhymes, but they do help to forge an extra link in the parent-child relationship. They also attract a toddler to words, through rhythm and rhyme.

Nursery rhymes and fairy stories

Nursery rhymes and songs are very often a toddler's first books. They have a story form, there is a rhythm in them, and often an accompanying tune that the parent knows.

Nursery rhymes have a particular magic of their own for toddlers. In effect, they are very short stories with rhythm and rhyme, and large, colourful pictures to talk about:

> Little Miss Muffet
> Sat on a tuffet...

Rhymes like Humpty Dumpty, Jack and Jill and Baa Baa Black Sheep also have tunes that are immediately recognisable. The combination of story, rhyme, tune and picture setting is irresistible to toddlers. Often nowadays, books of nursery rhymes and songs have accompanying cassettes which heighten interest.

Books of fairy stories also have large and brightly coloured pictures, so that Mum or Dad can sit with their child and allow conversation to develop about the pictures. "Is the giant really that big?" said John. "Yes," said Dad. "Look, I'll show you." He climbed on to a chair and breathed in deeply.

"Fee, fi, fo, fum..." he began in a deep, deep voice. John's eyes widened in wonder. The story had come alive to him, through the acting-out of one of the scenes. Every evening, the little boy begged for a re-reading.

Linking with other activity areas

Counting rhymes are very valuable aids to early maths activities. A parent can sit with her child, sing the rhyme, and make the actions.

"One, two, three,
Mother caught a flea,
Put it in a teapot
Made a cup of tea."

"One, two, three, four, five,
Once I caught a fish alive,
Six, seven, eight, nine, ten,
Then I let it go again."

"All good children, count together,
One, two, three, four, five."

Picture books and information books

The pictures in these books are of great importance, because they form discussion points. They need to be highly-coloured, and filled with interesting features. A parent can read the story, or key words, and run a finger along what is being read.

CHAPTER 7

Pre-reading

There are many activities that can serve as a practical basis for reading. These are:

- play with bath letters, solid letters, and letters that are magnetised;
- alphabet sets;
- looking at words in the street, the park, the shops, the supermarket;
- watching programmes for toddlers that animate letters and accompany them with letter sounds, e.g. *Sesame Street*, some CD-ROMS;
- ABC books that display a picture with the related letter word beneath;
- talking, being read to;
- listening to tapes, etc.
- rhymes, riddles and songs.

Play with letters

There are several types of play letters, from ones that can be stuck to the side of the bath, to large plastic ones for the toy box, to magnetic letters that stick to the front of the fridge. You do not need to say what the letter is, or its sound, but sooner or later a toddler will ask.

"What this?" asked Hannah, pulling a letter from the fridge. "That's an 'E'," said mum.

"What this?" asked Hannah, pulling off another letter, and so on.

Alphabet sets

To help your child learn the letters of the alphabet, there are sets of letters that can be fitted on to a board, rather like a jigsaw puzzle. However, these are really only within the manipulative range of an older toddler.

Looking at letters and words in real life

Getting your toddler to notice words and letters in the street, in shops, and in places you visit makes such trips more satisfying for an active mind:

"What's that say?" says Mark.
"It says 'Crofton Street'," I say.
A little later: "What's that say?"
"M. Simpson, Baker," I read.

Clearly, this is not part of a direct learning-to-read process, but it does generate interest in words. Soon she comes to realise that words have a meaning, that they tell you something about what is sold in a shop, or where someone lives.

Letters and words on objects such as tins of beans and packets of cereal sometimes lead a child to read. You should respond to your child's query when she asks what the written words say, e.g. "beans", "cornflakes", "cheese", and so on. Not all small children learn to read this way, but they still like to *know*.

Programmes that teach letter sounds

These include TV programmes such as *Sesame Street*, and other pre-school programmes, and a rapidly increasing number of CD-ROMS. Here, letters can be animated, to make the learning of letter sounds interesting. Toddlers who identify with a TV or book character will often sit for long periods listening.

ABC books

There are a wealth of ABC books on the market. They usually tie a letter to a word and picture, e.g. 'd' for dog. Just as you would use a picture book to read a story, these are books you can read with your toddler at bedtime, or when she is inclined to sit down and listen. They often become a toddler's favourite book.

Other activities

There are many other activities that contribute to a toddler's understanding, and become a valuable springboard for later reading activities. These include talking in general, being read to, listening to tapes of stories, and rhymes, riddles and songs.

These activities are dealt with in other chapters, and their contribution to the early learning of toddlers cannot be overestimated. Rhythm, rhymes and music form an invaluable background to words, word meanings and simple stories.

Toys and books for pre-reading

These include:

- bath letters, solid and magnetic letters;
- videos and CD-ROMS for pre-schoolers;
- ABC books;
- books and tapes of rhymes, riddles and songs.

CHAPTER 8
Manipulative skills

Manipulative skills include the ability to pick up, hold and move objects, and also the ability to co-ordinate physical movement.

The manipulative skills of a toddler improve naturally, but this process can be helped by:

- placing wooden bricks in towers, or end-to-end;
- fitting different sized plastic cups inside each other;
- building plastic ring towers;
- fitting shapes into corresponding holes in a posting box;
- activity centres;
- fitting jigsaw pieces together;
- cutting with safety scissors;
- using a thin crayon, pencil and paintbrush;
- learning to dress and undress doll's clothes (buttons, zips, etc);
- helping Mum and Dad put away shopping in cupboards, clothes in drawers, etc.
- general activities.

Playing with wooden bricks and plastic cups
Sadia is a young toddler. She sits on the floor with

crossed legs, and tries to build a tower with wooden bricks of the same size. She can build a two-brick tower easily, but the third brick is a problem. Eventually, she becomes frustrated, and throws the brick across the room.

Martin is an older toddler. He can just about build a seven- or eight- brick tower. Then, he deliberately collapses it, screaming with laughter.

Plastic cups that fit into each other to make a tower are also useful in manipulative play. Once you have shown your toddler how to fit them together, he can be left to experiment. Initially, however, this is a difficult activity. The fewer cups to fit together, the easier he finds it.

A similar toy to use in this type of play is a tower of plastic rings. The toddler fits each ring over the central stick, hopefully in order, from biggest to smallest. Ordering for size, however, is a difficult activity, so you need to have room, and probably some months, for experimentation.

The posting box and activity centre

This is an educational toy that can be purchased at more than one level of difficulty. Usually cylindrical or cuboid in shape, there are holes cut in the top to push 3-D shapes through. An easier posting box would have three holes for cuboid, prism and cylindrical shapes.

Andrew seemed to have the perfect answer to this

plastic-shapes-in-hole idea. He would take his little wooden hammer, and try to hammer any of the shapes through the nearest hole. However, he eventually progressed to five shapes quite quickly (without the use of the hammer!).

Activity centres are primarily for babies and very young toddlers. There are things to push, pull, move to the left, move to the right, and so on. With the movements are sounds, or colour and pattern changes.

Jigsaw puzzles

Fitting jigsaw pieces together is not entirely a manipulative skill. A certain amount of thought

has to go into matching patterns as well. An older toddler can often succeed with a seven- or eight-piece puzzle, if the pieces are large.

Crayons, pencils and paintbrushes

Chubby crayons can be used by young toddlers, because they do not demand too much manipulative skill. However, a toddler may find thin crayons, pencils and paintbrushes difficult to hold and guide across paper. It is best not to introduce these too early, or it could lead to frustration.

Cutting with scissors

Initially, this needs to be taught: "Hold the scissors like this, and cut like this." Always use safety scissors with young children. These have rounded ends. Being taught such a skill leads to the toddler being proud of his ability to do such things. "I am cut paper now", announced Anne to her grandparents. You will have to wait some time before your toddler can master this skill. Like holding and using a pencil, it takes time and patience.

Buttons, zips and Velcro

Putting on and taking off a teddy or doll's clothes, or dressing himself, can help your toddler with the difficult problem of fastening buttons, zips or Velcro. Such skills, like putting on socks and shoes, are learnt relatively easily, but others, like tying shoelaces, can take longer.

Learning skills like these increase a toddler's confidence in himself and, from that point of view alone, are extremely important.

Other skills

Other activities that develop manipulative abilities include:

- putting away spoons and forks in a drawer;
- putting clothes away in piles in drawers;
- laying the table;
- tidying up, including putting toys away in cupboards and boxes.

Toys to assist manipulative ability

- Activity centres;
- Safety scissors;
- Plastic cup sets;
- Wooden building bricks;
- Posting box;
- Graduated ring sets;
- Crayons, pencils, paintbrushes;
- Dolls' clothes with zips and buttons;
- Jigsaw puzzles.

CHAPTER 9
Solving practical problems

For a toddler, everyday activities, such as eating and dressing, are skills that have to be learned. For a toddler there are essentially two types of practical problems:

- those that arise out of real-life;
- those that a parent sets for a child, to stretch thinking.

Practical problems include:

- problems with dressing and undressing, hair-brushing;
- problems with using spoons, cups;
- problems in packing away clothes, shoes, toys;
- problems in sorting and matching;
- ordering problems;
- "bring me" problems;
- washing and cleaning problems.

Dressing and undressing

Typical problems include putting on jumpers; matching and putting on socks; pulling on trousers; putting shoes on the right feet; the doing-up of buckles, zips, buttons and laces; the fastening of poppers and Velcro.

Each of these problems can be turned into a game. Turning the jumper upside down and trying to pull it on your toddler that way, putting socks or shoes on hands instead of feet, will relax her, before you show her exactly how to do it. Words help: "This way up, put your head through the 'big' hole of the jumper." Or, "Lay the trousers down, like this, with the zip on top. Sit down at the top end, then pull them on, putting each foot down a hole."

Clearly, a toddler naturally becomes more competent at dressing with age, and it is important that you are patient. Doing up laces comes later. Explanations are important at every age, though, and a toddler always needs frequent encouragement in whatever little thing she

achieves. Use words such as "very good", or "well done", frequently.

Rukhsa always appeared with her slip-on shoes on the wrong feet, until her auntie pointed out that "the round part here goes on the outside of the foot".

Spoons and cups

Actions such as using a spoon properly to eat with, or a cup to drink with, are skills that need to be taught. A game that illustrates the *wrong* way to do it usually makes a toddler laugh, and takes tension out of the situation (e.g. drinking from the wrong side of the cup, or trying to eat beans with an upside-down spoon). This can be followed by "You show me." Remember that every small skill that you find easy needs to be learnt from scratch by your toddler; he needs to feel proud when a skill is learnt, like finding his cup, spoon and plate, and bringing them to the table.

Packing away toys, clothes and shoes

To put objects away in good order, as opposed to throwing them into a box, cupboard or drawer is a difficult problem for a toddler. He needs to order according to size and type of object. For example, in a drawer, socks will be separate from vests, and larger clothes are usually on the bottom, smaller ones on the top. Folding clothes is difficult, even for an older toddler, but this age group enjoys helping Mummy or Daddy to tidy up. Learning to put books into neat piles is a little easier, as long as the books are not too heavy.

Sorting and matching

This was mentioned in chapter 5. It involves sorting clothes into sensible groups, putting books in the 'right place'; matching gloves, shoes, socks into pairs; putting knives, forks and spoons into the correct kitchen drawer compartment; laying the table for dinner or tea; knowing where to find things, and where to put them away.

Such things are usually done with a parent, but with experience, on her own. Each activity is part skill learning and part problem solving. For Richard, this is his favourite activity. Unfortunately, he will now put away *any* clothes in cupboards and drawers, including those laid out for washing!

Wooden bricks

Using wooden bricks, it is possible to sort and match for colour, size and shape. If three green bricks and three red bricks are put in a pile, a toddler can be shown how to separate the colours: "these are green" and "these are red". Similarly, this can be repeated for two different *shapes* of brick, and two different *sizes*. These are difficult activities for many toddlers, however, and sorting and matching for colour needs to be done at a different time to sorting for shape or size.

Putting bricks in order

Even older toddlers can find ordering bricks for size, shape and colour difficult. For colour, this includes showing her how to arrange three red and three yellow bricks in various orders – for example, red / red / red, then yellow / yellow / yellow, or red / yellow / red / yellow / red / yellow. For size, this could be big / small / big / small. There are endless variations, including spoon / fork / spoon / fork. A parent needs to be careful, though, that the problem is not too taxing, or a toddler can feel frustrated.

"Bring me" problems

This adds an extra dimension to problem solving, because a parent is using spoken words alone to

explain the problem. For example, a parent can say, "Bring me a spoon from the drawer" or "Bring me your *blue* shoes from your cupboard upstairs." For young toddlers the instructions must be very simple: "Get your cup" or "Bring Teddy."

Washing and cleaning

These include using a facecloth to wash with, a hairbrush to brush hair, and a handbrush to sweep with. They begin as basic skills, and end up as problems to be solved: "Here is a cloth. See if you can clean the table." Other skills that can be learned at this age are polishing and dusting, and even washing up. Jason has been "washing up" since two-and-a-half, wearing a little plastic apron. He loves it to pieces.

Clear instructions

Problem-solving is a difficult area for a toddler. What might seem a simple task to a parent can be immensely daunting for a young child. Parents need to be extremely patient, and spell out a problem in clear language, and with a clear demonstration.

Toys for problem-solving

- Dolls for dressing and undressing;
- Wooden bricks of different sizes, shapes and colours;
- Plastic play tea sets.

CHAPTER 10

Visiting places of interest

Places a parent can take a toddler to include:

- shopping centres;
- the zoo;
- castles and historic houses;
- the seaside;
- interactive museums;
- fairs;
- pantomimes and other children's shows;
- the cinema – children's films (e.g. Disney);
- parks and playgrounds.

Choose from this list according to the age and interest of your child. It's a good idea to share information about local places of interest with other parents.

Shopping centres

As these centres get bigger, and have more varied retail outlets, a trip for a toddler becomes an adventure in itself. There are a myriad of interesting objects for parent to point out, pick up and name for him. Perhaps there is the chance of a ride on an electric children's car and a special treat at a café, or a soft-toy play centre.

The zoo

You can prepare for this trip by getting animal books from the library and the bookshop, and talking to your toddler about the animals on the day before. It helps to gather as much information about the zoo being visited, and to sit down and discuss the itinerary.   "Shall we see the elephants first, or the monkeys?"

Later, after the trip, you make a scrapbook of the visit, with cut-outs from the zoo material.

Castles and historic houses

A short visit to a castle or historic house is a visit into history, so you need to do a little preparation

on books, for example, on castles generally, and perhaps on that castle in particular. Pre-trip conversation only needs to be basic: "The soldiers fired arrows from these windows", and so on. As for the zoo trip, brochures and booklets purchased from the bookshop can be made into a scrapbook.

The seaside

A trip to the seaside is often the most memorable for a toddler. There are many interesting things and places to see on a beach, along the seafront, and in the various places of interest along the way.

Seaside towns often provide a wealth of publicity material, and this, in addition to the use of books, can help in your preparation for a trip. There are sand, stones, shells, a pier, the sea, fish, crabs, seaweed, rocks, seaside peppermint rock, mementos, Sea World (maybe), fair rides, but above all, the sounds, smells and sights. It is a magical place for a toddler to visit, and talk about afterwards.

Museums

These are often considered dull and dry places, but there is usually much to enliven a trip. Some museums have dinosaur, whale and shark mock-ups, and a little preparation and talking with a child can make him intrigued to see the size and form of these monsters. A brief look into history books can explain about Stone Age clothes, utensils and weapons; about Saxons, Vikings and

Normans. Afterwards, there is another scrapbook to make for him, and to write his name on.

Fairs

Apart from the thrill of toddler rides, there are rotating wheels and flashing coloured lights, halls of mirrors, and a unique world of sounds and smells.

After one visit, John's finger paintings became full of bright and vivid colours. "That's the fair", he said, and painted his interpretation of the Big Wheel, the Ghost Train, and the Big Dipper.

Pantomimes and other children's shows

Toddlers, particularly older toddlers, can be thrilled and entertained by the colour and knock-about humour of a pantomime. It is another valuable piece of experience to build into a child's early life; something to draw upon for later creative efforts, writing, and even investigative pieces.

Children's films

A toddler's imagination, his musical and story senses, are all stimulated by videos of Disney cartoons. The characters and songs are memorable, and the stories often gripping. Toddlers will watch films such as *The Lion King*, *Aladdin*, *The Jungle Book*, *Dumbo*, etc. and also non-Disney films like *The Wizard of Oz*, again and again.

Parks and playgrounds

Hardly a toddler has missed this experience – of climbing, sliding, swinging and going round and round on a roundabout. The movements and experiences from a playground are another memory on which later nursery and school experience will be built. The more varied and rich such experiences, the more extensive will be the learning at a later time.

CHAPTER 11

Any other problems?

It is a worry for parents if they feel that their toddler is not progressing at a 'normal' rate, either physically or mentally, or both. There may be no need for concern. Toddlers progress at their own personal rate of development, and some 'catch up' at a later age. However, if there is real concern, the health visitor, the family doctor and optician can arrange checks for any possible sight and hearing problems, and for possible physical causes of slow intellectual development.

Working parents may worry about the level and quality of stimulation their toddler receives. This should be a prime consideration when choosing a nursery or childminder. Ask for recommendations from other parents and explain your requirements clearly.

In addition, the following agencies will be pleased to advise you if you have worries about your child:

The Dyslexia Association

98 London Road
Reading
Berks RG1 5AU
Telephone 0118 966 8271

The Dyspraxia Foundation

8 West Alley
Hitchin
Herts SG5 1EG
Telephone 01462 454 986

The National Autistic Society

276 Willesden Lane
London NW2 5RB
Telephone 020 7833 2299

For parents who feel that their child needs more intellectual stimulation, contact:

The National Association for Gifted Children

Elder House
Elder Gate
Milton Keynes MK9 1KR
Telephone 01908 673 677

NSPCC

NSPCC National Centre
42 Curtain Road
London EC2A 3NH
Website: www.nspcc.org.uk

The National Society for the Prevention of Cruelty to Children (NSPCC) is the UK's leading charity specialising in child protection and the prevention of cruelty to children. It also operates the NSPCC Child Protection Helpline – a free, 24 hour service which provides counselling, information and advice to anyone concerned about a child at risk of abuse. The Helpline number is: 0808 800 5000, Textphone: 0800 056 0566.

Preschool Learning Alliance
69 King Cross Road
London WC1X 9LL
Childcare helpline 020 7837 5513

Child Accident Prevention Trust
18-20 Farringdon Lane
London EC1R 3HA
Telephone 020 7608 3828

The National Association of Toy and Leisure Libraries
68 Churchway
London NW1 1LT
Telephone 020 7387 9592
E-mail: admin@natll.ukf.net
Website: www.charitynet.org/~NATLL
Registered Charity Number 270291

Found throughout the UK, toy libraries offer services to local families based on regular toy loan for a nominal fee (and sometimes for free). Leisure Libraries provide recreational facilities for adults with learning difficulties.

We hope you enjoyed reading this book and would like to read other titles in the NSPCC range.

If you have any difficulty finding other titles you can order them direct (p&p is free) from Egmont World Limited, P O Box 7, Manchester M19 2HD.

Please make a cheque payable to Egmont World Limited and list the titles(s) you want to order on a separate piece of paper.

Please don't forget to include your address and postcode.

Thank you

... and remember every book purchased means another contribution towards the NSPCC cause.

NSPCC Child Care Guides   £2.99

First-time Parent, by Faye Corlett	0 7498 4669 0
Understanding Your Baby, by Eileen Hayes	0 7498 4670 4
Understanding Your Toddler, by Eileen Hayes	0 7498 4671 2
Toddler Talk and Learning, by Ken Adams	0 7498 4776 X
Sleeping Through the Night, by Faye Corlett	0 7498 4775 1
Bullying, by Sheila Dore	0 7498 4766 2
A Special Child in the Family, by Mal Leicester	0 7498 4673 9
Being Different, by Mal Leicester	0 7498 4765 4
Potty Training and Child Development, by Faye Corlett	0 7498 4763 8
Changing Families, by Sheila Dore	0 7498 4762 X
Positive Parenting, by Eileen Hayes	0 7498 4674 7
Bedtimes and Mealtimes, by Margaret Bamforth	0 7498 4672 0

NSPCC Learning Guides   £2.99
by Nicola Morgan

Get Ready for School	0 7498 4492 2
Reading and Writing at School	0 7498 4491 4

NSPCC Happy Kids Story Books   £2.99
by Michaela Morgan

Maya and the New Baby.	0 7498 4637 2
Spike and the Footy Shirt	0 7498 4636 4
Jordan and the Different Day	0 7498 4638 0
Jody and the Biscuit Bully	0 7498 4635 6
Emily and the Stranger	0 7498 4639 9
Happy Kids All Together Now	0 7498 4640 2